Picture the Past

Life in San Francisco's Chinatown

Sally Senzell Isaacs

Heinemann Library
Chicago, Illinois

Produced for Heinemann Library by
   Bender Richardson White.
Editor: Lionel Bender
Designer and Media Conversion: Ben White
Picture Researcher: Cathy Stastny
Production Controller: Kim Richardson

07 06 05 04 03
10 9 8 7 6 5 4 3 2 1

Printed and bound in the United States by Lake Book
Manufacturing, Inc.

Isaacs, Sally Senzell, 1950-
   Life in San Francisco's Chinatown / Sally Senzell Isaacs.
      p. cm. -- (Picture the past)
Summary: An overview of life for the Chinese immigrants
living in San Francisco from 1840 through 1910, including
their employment, family life, and everyday activities, as
well as the prejudice they faced.
Includes bibliographical references (p.   ) and index.
   ISBN 1-58810-692-6 (HC), 1-40340-524-7 (Pbk)
   1. Chinese Americans--California--San Francisco--History--
Juvenile literature. 2. Chinese Americans--California--San
Francisco--Social conditions--Juvenile literature. 3.
Chinatown (San Francisco, Calif.)--History--Juvenile
literature. 4. Chinatown (San Francisco, Calif.)--Social
conditions--Juvenile literature. 5. San Francisco (Calif.)--
History--Juvenile literature. 6. San Francisco (Calif.)--Social
conditions--Juvenile literature. (1. Chinese Americans--
California--San Francisco--History. 2. Chinese Americans--
California--San Francisco--Social conditions. 3. Chinatown
(San Francisco, Calif.)--History. 4. Chinatown (San Francisco,
Calif.)--Social conditions. 5. San Francisco (Calif.)--History.
6. San Francisco (Calif.)--Social life and customs.) I. Title.
   F869.S39 C535 2002
   979.4'61004951--dc21
                                    2002000791

Special thanks to Angela McHaney Brown at Heinemann
Library for editorial and design guidance and direction.

Acknowledgments
The producers and publishers are grateful to the following
for permission to reproduce copyright material:
California Historical Society: pages 15 (image FN-23076),
22 (image FN-08619), 27 (image FN-04760). Corbis Images:
Arnold Genthe, pages 19, 20, 21, 24. Lionheart Books:
page 30. North Wind Pictures: pages 7, 12, 13, 17, 23.
Peter Newark's American Pictures: pages 1, 3, 6, 9, 10, 14,
16, 26, 28.
Cover photograph: California Historical Society (FN-04760).

The publisher would like to thank Joyce Mao for her
comments in the preparation of this book.

Every effort has been made to contact copyright holders
of any material reproduced in this book. Omissions will be
rectified in subsequent printings if notice is given to the
publisher.

Illustrations on pages 4, 8, 11, 25, 29 by John James and
               James Field.
Map by Stefan Chabluk.

ABOUT THIS BOOK

This book tells about the daily life of San Francisco's Chinatown from 1848 to 1910. People from China began going to California in 1848. They took jobs digging gold and building railroad tracks. They moved to a small area of San Francisco to live among other people who spoke their language. In 1853, a newspaper writer labeled this area "Chinatown." There are Chinatowns in other American cities, including Los Angeles, New York, Chicago, and Boston. San Francisco's Chinatown is the oldest Chinese-American community.

We have illustrated the book with photographs of people and places from this time period. We have also included artists' ideas of how Chinese Americans lived in the late 1800s.

The Author
Sally Senzell Isaacs is a professional writer and editor of nonfiction books for children. She graduated from Indiana University, earning a B.S. degree in Education with majors in American History and Sociology. Sally Senzell Isaacs has written more than 30 history books for children.

Note to the Reader
Some words are shown in bold, **like this.** You can find out what they mean by looking in the glossary.

CONTENTS

The Rush for Gold

In 1847, most people in the world had never heard of California. Then, in January 1848, John Marshall discovered gold on John Sutter's land near Sacramento. Soon the news spread around the world. Within two years, 85,000 new people moved to California from all over the world. Everyone wanted gold! By 1852, more than 20,000 **immigrants** from China had arrived in California. Immigrants are people who move from another country to live in a new country.

Look for these
The illustration of a Chinese-American boy and girl shows you the subject of each double-page story in the book.
  The illustration of a Chinese lantern marks boxes with interesting facts about life in San Francisco's Chinatown.

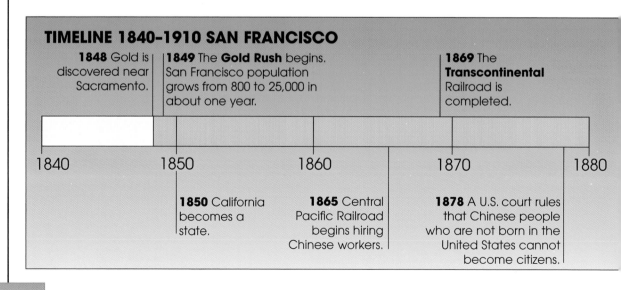

TIMELINE 1840–1910 SAN FRANCISCO

1848 Gold is discovered near Sacramento.

1849 The **Gold Rush** begins. San Francisco population grows from 800 to 25,000 in about one year.

1869 The **Transcontinental** Railroad is completed.

1840   1850   1860   1870   1880

1850 California becomes a state.

1865 Central Pacific Railroad begins hiring Chinese workers.

1878 A U.S. court rules that Chinese people who are not born in the United States cannot become citizens.

During the Gold Rush, many Americans rode horses and **stagecoaches** to California. Immigrants from China arrived by ships. Many landed in San Francisco. After 1869, they could ride trains from coast to coast.

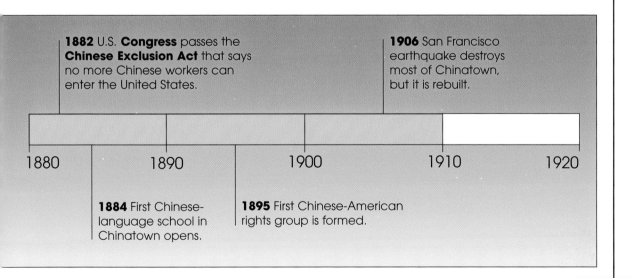

1882 U.S. **Congress** passes the **Chinese Exclusion Act** that says no more Chinese workers can enter the United States.

1906 San Francisco earthquake destroys most of Chinatown, but it is rebuilt.

1880   1890   1900   1910   1920

1884 First Chinese-language school in Chinatown opens.

1895 First Chinese-American rights group is formed.

Gold Mountain!

In China, life was not easy. Terrible floods ruined the farms. Then there were months without rain. Families were hungry and scared. Wars broke out throughout the country. People in China heard stories about California. The stories called California "Gold Mountain." Some stories said there were golden rocks the size of oranges!

Hundreds of ships landed in San Francisco. Most of the passengers were ready to search for gold. But some stayed in town to open stores and restaurants.

The Chinese among these passengers arriving in San Francisco filled out **immigration** forms. Then someone took them to a neighborhood where Chinese people lived. The neighborhood was called Chinatown.

Many Chinese men wanted to go to California, make money, and return to China to help their families. The 6,000-mile (9,600-kilometer) trip across the Pacific Ocean took two to three months. Passengers were crowded on the ships. The food was terrible, and there was little clean water. Many people got sick on the ships. Many died.

PLEASE COME!

Some businessmen sent ads to China. They offered free tickets on a ship to any men who wanted to become gold **miners.** The miners could pay them back, plus extra money, after they found gold. It could take eight to ten years to pay back the money.

The Gold Miners

From San Francisco, Chinese men took boats or **stagecoaches** into the hills. They set up tents or cheap wooden houses. They stayed until most of the gold was gone from that land. Then they moved to another place, or they went back to China.

Most **miners** did not know how to cook or wash clothes. The Chinese men did these jobs for everyone and earned money for it.

At first, American miners welcomed miners from other countries. But after a while, there was not much gold left in California. The Americans did not want to share it with people from other countries. They sent Chinese miners to areas where there were only bits of gold dust. Life was hard for Chinese workers. They mined for hours to get just a little gold.

Large groups of Chinese men work together. Some men shovel dirt into a box with tiny holes in the bottom. Another man pours water over the dirt. If there is any gold in the dirt, it stays in the box. The Chinese were hard workers.

The Railroad

Many towns were growing in California. Now the United States needed trains to carry people and supplies across the nation. The Central Pacific Railroad company started building tracks in Nebraska. The Union Pacific company started in California. The two tracks met in Utah. Workers from around the world came to work on the railroad.

About 12,000 Chinese men worked on the Central Pacific Railroad. They chopped trees, shoveled dirt, carted it away, drilled, and blasted through steep mountains. It was very hard work.

On May 10, 1869, the two tracks met in Promontory Point, Utah. Everyone celebrated the **Transcontinental** Railroad! Now there were train tracks from New York to California. The railroad could never have been built without the Chinese workers. They often had the most dangerous tasks.

This is the celebration in Promontory Point. The leaders of both railroad companies hammered a golden spike to join the train tracks. Using the Transcontinental Railroad, a person could travel across the country in just ten days.

Looking for Work

After the railroad was built, thousands of Chinese people were looking for jobs. There were not many jobs. Also, many Americans did not want to hire Chinese people. Some Chinese people opened stores in Chinatown. Others did work that many Americans did not want to do. They washed other people's **laundry.** They cooked food in restaurants. They cooked and cleaned in the homes of rich people.

This is Chinatown in 1880. The people in the lower left corner are doing laundry.

Some Chinese people collected rags to make paper. Others worked in **factories** and on farms. Chinese people took whatever jobs they could get. They even took less pay than American workers for the same work.

There were some Chinese **merchants** who traveled back and forth to China. They brought rice, tea, sugar, cloth, and tools to sell in San Francisco.

These people are keeping records of how much money their store is making. The man on the left is adding numbers using a traditional Chinese calculator called an abacus. He slides beads across rods in a wood frame.

"Stay Away"

By 1882, more than 300,000 Chinese people had moved to the United States. This was a difficult time in the country. There were not enough jobs. In California, thousands of Americans and **immigrants** had no jobs. And thousands more people were moving to California from eastern states. The farmers, too, were having a tough time. For two years, there was no rain. The fields dried up and there were no fruits or vegetables to eat or to sell.

Many Americans were angry with the Chinese people who had jobs. This cartoon shows an American washing machine company chasing away a Chinese man who owns a **laundry.**

The Exclusion Act was a sad thing for the Chinese in the United States. Now their wives, brothers, sisters, parents, and other relatives would not be able to join them from China.

In San Francisco, some citizens attacked Chinese people and burned their stores. The citizens of San Francisco passed several laws that hurt the Chinese people in other ways. In 1882, the U.S. **Congress** passed the **Chinese Exclusion Act.**

THE LAWS

Chinese people could not
- vote
- bring their families to the U.S.
- marry non-Chinese people
- become U.S. citizens.

The Chinese Exclusion Act said that no more Chinese workers could come to the United States for ten years.

Chinatown

In 1880, Chinatown took up twelve blocks of San Francisco. About 22,000 Chinese people lived there. They were mostly men. The streets were filled with bright signs made with fancy Chinese letters. The air was filled with the sound of several different Chinese languages. At night, candles flickered in paper lanterns. The people who lived there had brought many things from their home country.

Chinatown had stores of every kind. There were barbershops, butchers, tailors, vegetable stands, restaurants, and **laundries.** Stores sold tea, spices, and Chinese medicine. The store owners were Chinese and so were most of the customers.

16

The people of Chinatown worked very hard. After work, they enjoyed games called Fan-Tan, Pai Gow, and Mah-Jongg. They also enjoyed watching plays inside the two Chinese theaters in the neighborhood. A play could be very long, sometimes lasting more than a day.

MANNERS AT THE PLAY

The play was long, but people did not have to sit still. While watching a play, the audience could
- buy fruit and melon seeds to eat
- smoke
- walk around
- chat with friends.

The people had parades and parties as they did back in China. Many people marched through the streets under this colorful dragon.

The Family

Most Chinese men came to the United States alone. They did not have the money to bring a family. Since most men did not have their parents, wives, or children nearby, they formed family groups. Everyone with the same family name joined one group. These people helped each other in many ways. People also formed groups based on the communities in which they lived.

These Chinese men are praying inside a Chinese **temple.** The Americans, on the left, are watching.

Most children in Chinatown learned to speak Chinese from their parents. Some children never learned English. That made it hard for them to ever leave Chinatown.

THE FAMILY NAME

People in the United States say their family names after their personal names, such as Katie Smith. In China, people say their family names first, then their personal names.

The **Chinese Exclusion Act** allowed some people to come to the United States after 1882. They included teachers, **scholars,** and **merchants.** These people were also allowed to bring their wives and children with them. As those children grew up, they married and started new families.

Chinatown's Children

These children are watching someone write Chinese words. Instead of letters, the Chinese language has about 50,000 symbols. Each stands for a word or part of a word.

This is the Chinese symbol for *dog*.

Parents taught their children to work hard. If the parents owned a store or restaurant, the children worked there, too. Parents also wanted their children to learn to read and write. For many years, Chinese children were not allowed in **public schools.** Instead, they went to classes in churches and other places. By 1886, Chinese children were allowed in public school, but often they were not the same schools as white children attended.

TOYS

Chinese **immigrants** brought these toys to the United States:
- yoyos
- tops
- jump ropes
- kites
- Chinese checkers.

Chinese children often went to two schools. In public school, they learned to read and write English. They also learned math and geography. After school and on weekends, these children went to Chinese schools to learn to read and write in Chinese.

This man is selling toys on the streets of Chinatown. The children are very interested.

Toys such as yoyos and kites were popular in China before they were popular in the United States.

Homes

There were many kinds of places to live in Chinatown. Most of them were small and crowded with people. Some people lived in **apartment** buildings that were split into tiny rooms. Other lived in the backs of **factories** and restaurants. If people had little money to spend on furniture, they used wooden boxes as tables and chairs.

There are stores on the first floor of these buildings in Chinatown. People lived in apartments above the stores.

HOLIDAYS

Chinese Americans still celebrate holidays from China. These holidays include:
- The New Year (January or February)
- Lantern Festival (February)
- Dragon Boat Festival (May or June)
- Moon Festival (September or October).

To save money, many Chinese men would live in one room. They took turns sleeping in one bed. While one man worked, another slept in his bed.

Most of the buildings in Chinatown were made of wood. In 1906, an earthquake shook San Francisco. A fire broke out, and all of Chinatown burned to the ground. The people of San Francisco worked to rebuild almost everything that had been there.

Clothes

SHOE MAKERS

Some Chinese Americans sat on the sidewalk and made shoes for passing customers. Many others worked in shoe **factories.** In 1873, half of the shoes made in California were made by Chinese **immigrants.**

Although they lived in California, the people of Chinatown dressed as they did in China. The men wore baggy pants and long shirts. Women wore long dresses and jackets. By 1912, Chinese Americans started wearing American clothes. Even then, they wore Chinese clothes for holidays and celebrations, such as weddings.

Children and adults in Chinatown wore similar clothing. These adults are dressed to go to a Chinese wedding celebration.

All Chinese men wore their hair in a long, braided pigtail. That was a law in China. Chinese men in the United States kept their pigtails so they would be allowed to return to China. The pigtail was called a "queue," pronounced "Q."

HAIR STYLES

In 1911 in China, there was a war against the leader of the country. A man named Sun Yat-sen became China's new leader. He told all men to cut off their queues. In the United States, Chinese men cut theirs, too.

Food

The first **miners** from China introduced Americans to Chinese food. While other miners cooked beans and potatoes, the Chinese cooked rice with vegetables. The Chinese people stayed healthy because of this good food.

These men are eating dumplings, which are pieces of dough filled with meat or vegetables. They pick up the food with wooden sticks, called chopsticks.

Breakfast, lunch, and dinner were very similar. People ate lots of rice, noodles, and soups. Every meal might have vegetables, mushrooms, bamboo shoots, and small pieces of fish, beef, chicken, or pork. These meals were cheap and they did not take long to cook. Most food was cooked quickly in a bowl-shaped pot called a wok.

CHINESE FOOD

- Bing (pancake)
- Gao (doughnut)
- Mien (noodles)
- Tang (soup).

Chinatown had several stores for buying vegetables, rice, noodles, fish, and meat. These big bags are filled with rice.

27

Chinese Restaurants

Many of the first men in Chinatown stayed in places with beds but no kitchens. To eat, they went to restaurants. Many Chinese families earned money by cooking and selling Chinese food. Mothers, fathers, and children worked in the restaurants. The delicious food is still popular with Chinese people and people from other countries.

The Chinese restaurant was a place to eat and to share stories with friends.

Chinatown Recipe—Fortune Cookies

People in China did not make fortune cookies. They were first made in the United States in the early 1900s to bring people to Chinatown restaurants. Before you start the recipe, write good-luck fortunes on strips of paper about 2" by 1/2" (50 by 25 millimeters). Use waterproof ink. WARNING: Do not cook anything unless there is an adult to help you. Always ask an adult to use the oven and to handle hot foods.

YOU WILL NEED
- 1 cup (120 g) sifted flour
- 1 teaspoon salt
- 2 tablespoons cornstarch
- 6 tablespoons sugar
- 7 tablespoons vegetable oil
- 2 egg whites
- 3 tablespoons water
- 12 to 14 fortunes

FOLLOW THE STEPS

1. Preheat the oven to 350 degrees Fahrenheit (175 degrees Celsius).

2. Mix the flour, salt, cornstarch, and sugar in a large bowl. Add the oil and egg whites. Stir until smooth. Then add water and blend well.

3. Place 1 tablespoon of batter for each cookie on a greased cookie sheet (six cookies per sheet). Press the batter so each circle is about 3 inches (8 centimeters) wide and very thin.

4. Bake for 5 to 10 minutes or until edges are slightly brown.

5. (Be sure an adult helps with this step because the cookies will be very hot.) Put a fortune in the center of each cookie and fold the cookie over the fortune.

6. Put each cookie in a muffin tin with the open edge up. Let it cool. Repeat with remaining batter. This recipe makes between 12 and 14 fortune cookies.

Chinatown Today

Chinatown is still a lively neighborhood. Today it takes up many city blocks with homes, stores, schools, a hospital, restaurants, churches, **temples,** and more. Many Chinese Americans have left Chinatown to live in other parts of San Francisco, California, and the United States. And yet, many **immigrants** still come to Chinatown to live in a place that is both Chinese and American.

Thousands of people from around the world visit San Francisco every day. Chinatown is one of the most popular places to visit. Chinese Americans welcome guests to eat in their restaurants, shop in their stores and watch their colorful parades.

Glossary

apartment one of many rooms or sets of rooms within a building in which people live

Chinese Exclusion Act law passed in 1882 saying that no more workers from China could come to the United States for ten years. The law was extended for a longer period

Congress part of the United States government that makes laws

factory building where things are made in large numbers or amounts

Gold Rush starting in 1849, the time when people went to California to find gold

immigrant person who moves from another country to live in a new country

immigration moving from one country to another

laundry clothes that need washing; or, a place where workers wash and iron clothes for money

merchant person who buys and sells things

miner person who digs in the earth get valuable stones, such as gold

Native Americans first people living in America. They were here before explorers or settlers from Europe.

public school free school paid for by taxes (money paid by people to the government)

scholar person who has studied a subject for a long time

slave person who is owned by another person and is usually made to work for the person

stagecoach boxlike car pulled by horses in which people travel long distances

temple building used for prayer and worship

transcontinental across a continent, such as North America

More Books to Read

Goldin, Barbara Diamond. *Red Means Good Fortune: A Story of San Francisco's Chinatown.* New York: Puffin, 1996.

Olson, Kay Melchisedech. *Chinese Immigrants: 1850–1900.* Minnetonka, Minn.: Capstone Press, 2001.

Schanzer, Rosalyn. *Gold Fever!: Tales from the California Gold Rush.* Washington, D.C.: National Geographic Society, 1999.

Index